LISTENING FOR GOD
THROUGH
1 & 2 TIMOTHY
AND
TITUS

Lectio Divina Bible Studies

wph wesleyan
publishing
house

Indianapolis, Indiana

Beacon Hill Press of Kansas City
Kansas City, Missouri

Copyright © 2006 by Wesleyan Publishing House
Published by Wesleyan Publishing House and Beacon Hill Press of Kansas City
Indianapolis, Indiana 46250
Printed in the United States of America

ISBN-13: 978-0-89872-322-9
ISBN-10: 0-89827-322-6

Written by Donna Brayerton.

ABOUT THE
LECTIO DIVINA
BIBLE STUDIES

ectio divina, Latin for *divine reading,* is the ancient Christian practice of communicating with God through the reading and study of Scripture. Throughout history, great Christian leaders including John Wesley have used and adapted this ancient method of interpreting Scripture. This Bible study builds on this practice, introducing modern readers of the Bible to the time-honored tradition of "listening for God" through His Word. In this series, the traditional *lectio divina* model has been revised and expanded for use in group Bible study. Each session in this study includes the following elements. (Latin equivalents are noted in italics.)

- Summary   A brief overview of the session.
  Epitome

- Silence   A time of quieting oneself prior to
  Silencio   reading the Word.

- Preparation
  Praeparatio

  Focusing the mind on the central theme of the text.

- Reading
  Lectio

  Carefully reading a passage of Scripture.

- Meditation
  Meditatio

  Exploring the meaning of the Bible passage.

- Contemplation
  Contemplatio

  Yielding oneself to God's will.

- Prayer
  Oratio

  Expressing praise, thanksgiving, confession, or agreement to God.

- Incarnation
  Incarnatio

  Resolving to act on the message of Scripture.

The Lectio Divina Bible Studies invite readers to slow down, read Scripture, meditate upon it, and prayerfully respond to God's Word.

CONTENTS

INTRODUCTION

Picture an elderly, weathered Apostle Paul. He's been jailed and released and jailed again, shipwrecked, rescued, flogged, lauded, and derided. His days are dwindling to a precious few. Yet amidst his suffering, the thought of those he has discipled, those who will carry the mission and the vision to the next generation, warms him.

He has fought the good fight and is finishing the race. But issues still exist. Problems still need to be handled. His colleagues, friends who have taken up the mantle of ministry, need encouragement, strengthening, direction, and hope.

This is the backstory of the creation of the epistles 1 & 2 Timothy and Titus. Their recipients were two young pastors whom Paul left to minister to key groups of believers. Paul considered Timothy a spiritual son, a partner who had proven himself loyal and faithful even when the motives of other ministers proved less than honorable. Timothy led the church at Ephesus. Titus oversaw a young congregation in Crete. The early church knew these letters as the "Pastoral Epistles."

These were likely the last of Paul's New Testament letters to be written—circa AD 62–64, just prior to his death in Rome at the hands of the Emperor Nero. The chronological ordering of these epistles would be 1 Timothy, Titus, and then 2 Timothy.

Both 1 Timothy and Titus deal with issues of church administration and were particularly designed to strengthen the young leaders as they combated persecution and false teachers. 2 Timothy contains the warm, final words of a loving mentor to a dear friend. Paul warned Timothy to be careful, to be strong, and to be faithful to the end. At the precipice of martyrdom, Paul pointed both Timothy and Titus to the true source of salvation: "The Lord will rescue me from every evil attack and will bring me safely to his heavenly kingdom. To him be glory for ever and ever. Amen" (2 Timothy 4:18).

The last words of the Apostle Paul—the warnings and wisdom of these three letters—warrant close attention still today.

LIVING BY GOD'S GRACE

Listening for God through 1 Timothy 1:1–17

SUMMARY

Regrets are common to everyone. Past mistakes are hard to forget and can keep us from becoming all that God desires. Guilt-ridden people often find themselves endlessly trying to repay God for His grace and mercy. The impossibility of repayment leaves their attempts futile. But God's plan is not to keep us bound to regretful memories. He can use even our past mistakes for His glory.

The Apostle Paul was a man who had rejected Christ and become an enemy of the church. But God had other plans for him. After Paul received God's grace, he became an effective tool in God's hands despite his sordid past.

God's will is that each of us live in His abundant grace. He wants us to find our true liberty in Christ. This can only happen as we forsake a legalistic mindset and leave our past in God's hands.

SILENCE ✝ LISTEN FOR GOD

Meditate on the truth that God loves you not because of who you are or what you have done but because of who He is. God's love is unconditional.

PREPARATION ✝ FOCUS YOUR THOUGHTS

Does the memory of past failures hinder you or propel you in your faith walk? Why?

What are some ways we try to repay God for His mercy?

READING ✝ HEAR THE WORD

Paul wrote this letter to Timothy, a young pastor and son in the faith. Paul considered Timothy a trusted colleague. He had added Timothy to his missionary team on his second missionary journey. (See Acts 16:1–3.) His purpose in writing this letter was to encourage Timothy whom he had left to pastor the church in Ephesus. As you read, note how certain troubling issues within that local congregation are addressed.

Paul refers to his past as an enemy of the church in this passage. Read Acts 7:59–8:3 and Acts 9:1–6 for more background regarding his life prior to his conversion.

Note some key words in this passage:

Apostle: Literally, this means "one sent."

Grace: God's unmerited favor. Grace is God's full expression of love and joy given to one who is undeserving. It is God's strength and ability evidenced in the life of a believer.

Mercy: This is God's compassion extended to man. It specifically deals with His lovingkindness, which covers the consequences of our failures.

False doctrines: These were erroneous teachings not specifically stated in this passage but most likely related to the Law or Torah. Certain teachers were trying to bring believers back into the bondage of Old Testament legalism.

Read 1 Timothy 1:1–17.

Meditation ✦ Engage the Word

Meditate on 1 Timothy 1:1–2

Paul began this letter by calling himself an apostle of Christ Jesus. Who does he believe called him to this position?

Whom does God call today? Is the calling of God only for those in full-time Christian ministry or are all believers called by the command of God? In what ways do you believe God has sent you to represent Him?

What does Paul want Timothy to experience? (See v. 2.) In what ways are grace, mercy, and peace related? Why is it important for believers to experience this threefold blessing? What robs the believer of this blessing?

Meditate on 1 Timothy 1:3–11

Why did Paul leave Timothy in Ephesus? What kind of situation did Timothy walk into?

Certain teachers in Ephesus were stirring up controversies attempting to bring people back into Old Testament legalism.

They used myths and endless genealogies to make their case and cover over the truth of the gospel of grace. Their teachings kept people in bondage to Pharisaical laws. Why do you think they worked so hard to do this?

> It is said that truth is often eclipsed but never extinguished.
>
> –Titus Livius

Read the sidebar quote from Titus Livius, a Roman historian. The false teachers were trying to eclipse the truth but were unable to extinguish it. In what ways is the truth of the gospel eclipsed today?

Paul explains in verse 9 the proper use for the law. List the types of people for whom the law was intended. (See v. 9 and 10.) What would the law do for these people?

> The "currency" of our morality and good deeds is worthless in God's sight. Furthermore, we all are so heavily in debt to Him because of our sin that there is no question of our even partially paying our way with God.
>
> –Jerry Bridges

Read sidebar quote from Jerry Bridges. What are some ways Christians try to "spend the 'currency' of their own morality and good deeds"? What attitudes lead us to attempt to repay God for what He has done for us? Why is it impossible for us to even pay back a part of what we owe? How can we begin to let go of a recip-rocal mindset and live in the grace of God instead?

Meditate on 1 Timothy 1:12–17

Paul was once an enemy of the church and of Jesus Christ. What three things does he call himself in verse 13? How did he display each of these characteristics in his past life? (See Acts 9:1–9.) What is the reason Paul gives for his actions? Why would he have considered himself the worst of all sinners?

Focusing on your failures will always produce despair. How has Paul changed his thinking? (See verse 14.) Note the dramatic contrast he is making between himself and God. What characteristics does Paul see in the Lord?

Why did God show Paul His mercy? How is Paul's life an example to others?

Paul did not allow his past failures to keep him from being used by God. Rather he saw them as opportunities to display God's grace to others. How was this possible?

Read the sidebar quote from Oswald Chambers. What are some failures in your life that are obstacles keeping you from becoming all God intends you to be? Why haven't you allowed yourself to completely let the past sleep and receive God's grace?

> Our yesterdays present irreparable things to us; it is true that we have lost opportunities which will never return, but God can transform this destructive anxiety into a constructive thoughtfulness for the future. Let the past sleep, but let it sleep on the bosom of Christ.
>
> —Oswald Chambers

CONTEMPLATION ✝ REFLECT AND YIELD

Have you received God's transforming grace, or are you trying to repay Him for His mercy by living under your own self-imposed law?

If you would completely accept God's grace, how would your view of yourself change? How would your life change?

Will you allow God to use your past failures for His glory today?

Oratio PRAYER ✝ RESPOND TO GOD

In silence, close your eyes and see yourself placing the negative experiences of your life into a basket. Then see yourself giving that basket to the Lord. Hear His words of encouragement as you do this.

Incarnatio INCARNATION ✝ LIVE THE WORD

Read the sidebar quote from Rick Warren. List a few of your failures that you might share with others to help them in their journeys to God. Pray that God would show you specific people with whom you can share these experiences this week.

> The very experiences that you have resented or regretted most in life—the ones you've wanted to hide and forget— are the experiences God wants to use to help others. For God to use your painful experiences, you must be willing to share them. You have to stop covering them up, and you must honestly admit your faults, failures and fears.
>
> —Rick Warren

QUALITIES OF A GODLY LEADER

Listening for God through 1 Timothy 3:1–16

SUMMARY

For many churches today, finding qualified leaders is almost an impossible task. Some congregations are so in need of leaders that they place anyone willing to serve into key positions. Often, these people are too young in the faith or not living exemplary Christian lives. This contributes to unhealthy and problem-ridden local congregations.

The church in Ephesus where Timothy pastored was having similar problems. Paul understood that healthy churches need leaders who consistently display integrity of heart and mind.

Every person is a leader in some respect—whether at home, at work, in the community, or in church. Therefore, the attributes of a good leader should be the goal of every Christian. Each believer should strive to live a life worthy of his calling as God's very own. As you study this passage, allow the Holy Spirit to search your heart and examine your life.

SILENCE ✝ LISTEN FOR GOD

Jesus refered to Himself as bread sent from Heaven. Hear the voice of God calling you to eat of His Word—true heavenly Manna.

PREPARATION ✝ FOCUS YOUR THOUGHTS

What qualities do you believe are essential for a godly leader? What problems result in placing unqualified persons in leadership?

READING ✝ HEAR THE WORD

One of Paul's major concerns is the selection of leaders. In this passage the qualifications for church leaders are clearly outlined. Note not only the positive qualities which should be present in a leader's life, but also the negative qualities that should be absent.

Some important terms in this passage are as follows:

Overseer: Literally meaning "one who cares for another," this term generally refers to the role we would now call *pastor*. Also see Titus 1:6–9 for the requirements of this position.

Husband of one wife: The broadest interpretation of this phrase is someone who is faithful to his wife. Some believe it refers to a monogamous relationship. Others believe it speaks of someone who has never been previously married.

Deacon: This literally means *servant*. Some churches believe this refers to any lay ministry. Others see this as a specific ministry such as serving on a local church board or overseeing church property. The men chosen in Acts 6 were called deacons.

Wives: This also can be translated *women*. Some believe this refers to the wives of deacons; others believe it refers to women serving in leadership positions as deaconesses. The word *likewise* in this context seems to indicate that these women are leaders in the church.

Note, also, that verse 16 was probably a well-known hymn in the first-century church.

Read 1 Timothy 3:1–16.

MEDITATION ✝ ENGAGE THE WORD

Meditate on 1 Timothy 3:1–7

In what ways is the desire to be an overseer or pastor a noble task? The position of overseer is one of great honor but also great responsibility. If each individual member in the congregation would give proper respect to this position, what might change within the local church?

A list of qualifications necessary to be an overseer begins in verse 2. List these qualifications and define them in your own words. Which one of these characteristics do you feel is most important? Why?

Why is being able to manage one's own family such an important quality?

What kinds of problems might arise by placing a recent convert in this position?

Why is it important for leaders to have a good reputation with the unsaved in their communities?

Read the sidebar quote from Henry and Richard Blackaby. Churches measure spiritual leaders in many ways. How are you currently evaluating your leaders—by their accomplishments or by their spiritual fruit? Is it possible to have great accomplishments without being a true spiritual leader? Why or why not?

The unmistakable mark of leaders who are authenticated by God is that they are like Christ. They function in a Christ-like manner and those who follow them become more like Christ. The success of a spiritual leader is not measured in dollars, percentages, numbers, or attendance. A person is truly a spiritual leader when others are moved to be more like Christ.

—Henry and Richard Blackaby

As you review these biblical qualifications, note that a high standard has been placed on those who hold this position. Perhaps we should view these qualifications as goals to be reached rather than expecting our leaders to be perfect in these areas. What can you as a member of your church do to encourage and support your local pastor(s) in reaching this goal?

Meditate on 1 Timothy 3:8–13

The word *deacon* means *servant*. What kinds of servant roles do you have in your local church?

List the qualifications necessary for a deacon. Which of these qualifications are the same as that of an overseer? Which are different?

Why is it important that servants in the church first be tested? What practical ways can we use to measure their lives?

What are the requirements listed for being a woman leader in the church? Why are these qualities so important?

Do you believe the characteristics listed for deacons and for women leaders solely apply to those in leadership roles? Which qualifications should apply to everyone in the church? How can we encourage one another to reach these goals?

What do those who serve the church gain according to verse 13? Note that they obtain a blessing in their standing in the church as well as a personal blessing. Which of these do you think is more valuable? Why are both important?

Meditate on 1 Timothy 3:14–16

What does the Apostle Paul call the church in verse 15? How is the church both a pillar and a foundation of the truth?

Read the sidebar quote from Matthew Henry. It is important for leaders to strive to live like Christ so they are not counterproductive in ministry. What role do leaders play in helping a church body become a pillar and foundation of truth?

> Those who teach by their doctrine must teach by their life, or else they pull down with one hand what they build up with the other.
>
> —Matthew Henry

Paul ends this section by drawing our attention back to the Lord. Take each of the phrases in verse 16 and explain its meaning. Of what value are these in pursuing the goal of becoming a pillar and foundation of truth?

Why is it important that we keep our eyes on Christ rather than putting leaders under a microscope? What can we do as church members to help bring about this balance?

CONTEMPLATION ✞ REFLECT AND YIELD

What would happen in your church if more people were less critical and more encouraging to their leaders?

Churches are always looking for leaders. What might God be calling you to do within your local congregation? What is one leadership characteristic you want to cultivate in your life?

PRAYER ✞ RESPOND TO GOD

Read the sidebar quote from E.M. Bounds. In silence, pray that your pastors and leaders become people of prayer. Listen to what God is saying regarding how you can better support them. Hear His voice challenge you to live out the attributes of a godly leader.

> Men are God's method. The church is looking for better methods; God is looking for better men. What the church needs today is not more machinery, not new organizations or more and novel methods, but men who the Holy Spirit can use—men of prayer, men mighty in prayer.
>
> –E. M. Bounds

INCARNATION ✝ LIVE THE WORD

Make a list of your church leaders. Pray for them regularly using this Scripture as a basis for your prayers.

If you feel God calling you to a particular leadership role, have Christian friends pray with you to confirm God's will for your life. Then discuss this with your pastor.

KEEPING MONEY
IN PERSPECTIVE

Listening for God through 1 Timothy 6:6–21

SUMMARY

Money is a central focus of our society. Whether rich or poor, we find ourselves constantly bombarded with thoughts about our material wealth. Television programs fill the airwaves with ways for us to manage and spend our money. Advertisements entice us to overspend. Real-time stock quotes pop up on our computers and even our cell phones. Investment hustlers are constantly misleading people with get-rich-quick schemes.

Jesus knew money would be a major obstacle to those who desired to follow Him. He taught extensively on the subject of material wealth. In fact, in the Synoptic Gospels one out of every six verses relates to money, and sixteen of Christ's parables address the use of money.

It is easy to allow money to control us rather than our controlling it. As we study Paul's final thoughts in his first letter to Timothy, let us re-examine our own attitudes toward money.

SILENCE ✝ LISTEN FOR GOD

God has identified Himself as *El Shaddai*—the God who provides. In silence, meditate on the truth that God supplies your every need.

PREPARATION ✝ FOCUS YOUR THOUGHTS

Read the sidebar quote from Martin Luther. What do you think Luther meant by the "conversion of the purse"?

> There are three conversions necessary: the conversion of the heart, [the] mind, and the purse.
>
> —Martin Luther

Why is it so difficult for Christians to make Christ the Lord of their money?

Lectio READING ✝ HEAR THE WORD

As Paul concluded this letter, he focused on the universal principle of wealth. As you read, pay close attention to the verbs used in this passage. Also note the contrasts between the godly life and a life spent acquiring worldly wealth.

This passage discusses true contentment, which we can only find when we totally rely upon God as our Source. See Philippians 4:11–13 for a broader perspective on this important subject.

In 1 Timothy 6:10 it is not money itself, but one's attitude toward money, that leads to evil (literally, *all evils*).

In this passage you will encounter the following terms:

Godliness: This word is used nine times throughout this epistle. It refers not only to a holy attitude, but holiness as it is demonstrated.

Contentment: This refers to finding complete sufficiency, needing no other support or aid.

Fall: In this context, falling refers to being entrapped or overwhelmed by something.

Plunge: More specifically, here, this means to sink or drown.

Fight: This term used to refer to competing for a prize, implies the idea of agonizing over something.

Take hold: This calls for the believer to keep pursuing something and to seize it with a firm grip.

Read 1 Timothy 6:6–21.

MEDITATION ✝ ENGAGE THE WORD

Meditate on 1 Timothy 6:6–10

We live in a discontented society. What cultivates this discontent? How is "godliness accompanied by contentment" great gain? What do we lose when we are not content?

How does focusing on the fact that we cannot take our wealth with us when we die give us a different perspective regarding riches?

Paul defines our basic needs as food and clothing. How would you define the basic needs of life? Why are we often discontented even when these things are supplied?

Read the sidebar quote from Charles Spurgeon. Do you agree with this statement? Why or why not? How do we acquire true contentment?

> You say, "If I had a little more, I should be very satisfied."
> You make a mistake. If you are not content with what you have, you would not be satisfied if it were doubled.
> –Charles Haddon Spurgeon

Can a desire to be financially secure blot out our dependence on God? Explain.

In what ways can the desire for material things overwhelm us? What kinds of traps or temptations do people who are driven to acquire wealth fall into?

Do you believe Paul is saying that it is wrong to be rich, or to want to be rich? In what ways does the love of money lead to evil? How could this cause us to wander from our faith and cause grief?

Meditate on 1 Timothy 6:11–16

In the middle of his discussion on wealth, Paul interjected a solemn charge to young Timothy. What are the two things he told him to do? (See verse 11.) Note the verbs *pursue* and *flee*.

What did he want Timothy to flee from?

Many of the false teachers were probably financially secure. Why would it be important for Timothy to keep himself free from pursuing financial gain?

How do finances become a stumbling block to those in full-time Christian ministry today?

In 1 Timothy 5:17–18, Paul states that those in ministry should be taken care of financially. Why is it especially important that Christian workers receive proper support?

List the things verse 11 tells us we are to pursue and define each one. How will following after these things keep us from the love of money?

In what ways is the Christian life like competing for a prize? What does Paul mean by "fight the good fight of faith"?

Most scholars believe the confession Paul was referring to in verse 12 is Timothy's confession of Christ as Lord at his baptism. It is interesting to note that Paul compared Timothy's good confession to that of Christ's confession before Pontius Pilate (Mark 15:1–2). How are their confessions similar? How can our use of money testify to our faith?

Meditate on 1 Timothy 6:17–21

What are the commands given to those rich in material wealth? List the negative commands as well the positive commands in this section.

What negative attitudes can the rich easily fall into? How can wealth lead to prideful attitudes? Why is it perilous to put your hope in money? In whom should our hope be placed? Why?

Read the sidebar quote from John Wesley. In what ways is hoarding our wealth being like Judas Iscariot? Why would Wesley have more hope for Judas than for one who is miserly?

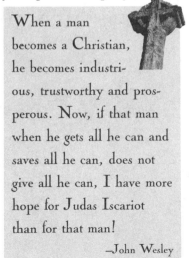

When a man becomes a Christian, he becomes industrious, trustworthy and prosperous. Now, if that man when he gets all he can and saves all he can, does not give all he can, I have more hope for Judas Iscariot than for that man!

—John Wesley

What does a generous spirit deposit in one's spiritual account? (See verse 19.) How does giving something away help us take hold of true life?

CONTEMPLATION ✝ REFLECT AND YIELD

On a scale from one to five—five being completely content— how would you rate your current feelings of contentment? Why?

In what ways have you fallen into the "love of money" trap?

What material things are you holding tightly? How does this hinder you from experiencing true life?

Prayer ✝ Respond to God

Read the quote from Ross J. Robert and then pray silently, allowing God to help you look at your heart through your pocketbook. Ask God to show you ways you can better serve Him through your wealth.

> To meet Jesus is to look yourself in the pocketbook, which is the most unmistakable way of looking yourself in the heart.
> —Ross J. Robert

Incarnation ✝ Live the Word

This week review your checkbook and analyze the current use of your wealth. Review your spending habits. How can you better use your wealth for God's Kingdom?

DON'T GIVE UP!

Listening for God through 2 Timothy 1:1–18

SUMMARY

Everyone has felt like quitting at one time or another. Discouragement can lead to defeat if you let it. It certainly can keep you from fulfilling God's will in your life.

As you read chapter 1 of Paul's second letter to Timothy, note the tone in this letter. It would seem that Timothy had become discouraged and was starting to lose heart. We can only surmise what could have contributed to this state of heart and mind. His beloved father in the faith, Paul, was in prison and facing death. The church in Asia was in the midst of great persecution. Emperor Nero had burned Rome and blamed Christians in order to turn public opinion against those believing in Christ.

Perhaps you, too, have faced situations where you thought about giving up. Maybe you feel like that today. Read on to discover how you can remedy this state of mind and remain faithful amid great discouragement.

SILENCE ✝ LISTEN FOR GOD

God understands when we feel like quitting. Pause and listen to the voice of God encouraging you to hold on to Him.

PREPARATION ✝ FOCUS YOUR THOUGHTS

Share a time in your life when you felt like giving up. What helped you to keep going?

Why is passion an important attribute for a Christian?

READING ✝ HEAR THE WORD

As you read this passage, remember that the Apostle Paul was imprisoned. He was facing the probability of death. This might be his last opportunity to encourage Timothy. The long-standing and intimate relationship between Paul and Timothy had brought comfort and strength to both of them.

Note Paul's specific instructions to Timothy in this passage. Pay attention to the things he wants Timothy to recall. These include his spiritual heritage, his ordination, Paul's faithfulness through suffering, and the teaching he received.

Here are some important terms in this section:

Clear conscience: This refers to an attitude of the heart. Paul is not stating that his actions were always perfect.

Sincere faith: This refers to a faith without hypocrisy.

Timidity: While this means having a fearful spirit, it can also mean giving in to intimidation.

Herald: This would refer to a crier, proclaimer, or preacher.

Onesiphorus: His name means *benefit bringing* or *profit-bearing*.

Read 2 Timothy 1:1–18.

MEDITATION ✟ ENGAGE THE WORD

Meditate on 2 Timothy 1:1–6

In this section Paul affirms his loving relationship with Timothy. List the ways he expresses their special bond. Why is it important for us to have close, reciprocal relationships with other Christians? How can these relationships be an encouragement in times of trouble?

Lois and Eunice passed down a living faith to Timothy. Why is it important to give a spiritual heritage to our children and grandchildren? Why do you suppose Paul used the memory of this heritage to help hearten the discouraged Timothy?

Read the sidebar that contains information from a Barna Group survey. What can we do as individuals to pass on a spiritual heritage to our young people? How can an early faith be an encouragement in times of stress?

Meditate on 2 Timothy 1:7–14

Paul reminds Timothy to "fan into flame" the gift of God. It brings to mind embers that have not entirely gone out.

The Barna Group recently published the results of a survey that shows that 64 percent of the Christians surveyed made their commitment to Christ before their eighteenth birthday; 13 percent made their profession of faith between the ages of 18 to 21; and only 23 percent received Christ after the age of 21. They also stated that people who become Christians before their teen years are more likely to remain "absolutely committed" to Christianity than those who are converted when older.

—The Barna Group, Ltd.

Read the sidebar quote from Jim Elliott. What things can become the asbestos in our lives? How can we re-ignite our passion for Christ when we become discouraged?

> Am I ignitable? God deliver me from the dread asbestos of "other things." Saturate me with the oil of the Spirit that I may be aflame.
>
> —Jim Elliot

Describe the characteristics of the Spirit God gives, as listed in verse 7. How would you define each of these characteristics? Why are all of these characteristics necessary?

How could shame contribute to discouragement? Paul strongly admonishes Timothy not to be ashamed to testify about the Lord. What causes Christians to be ashamed to testify about their faith?

Why is it important to remember that we have been called by God's purpose and grace rather than our own strength? How can this motivate us when we are tempted to give up?

Verses 9 and 10 give us the key points of the gospel message. List at least five of these points. Why would Paul remind Timothy to remember the gospel message? (Sometimes it is imperative that we go back to the basics to regain perspective when going through hard times.)

What are the three terms Paul uses to describe his calling in verse 11. How can each of us be a herald, apostle, and teacher? Look back at the definitions introduced earlier for clues.

Why isn't Paul ashamed, even though he is in prison? How does a firm conviction regarding Christ keep us from throwing in the towel when we are discouraged?

Read the sidebar quote from Chuck Swindoll. How are attitude and passion related? Why is a positive attitude imperative to remain ablaze for God?

What is Paul's final instruction to Timothy in this section? (See verse 14.) From the context it would seem that this good deposit is the sound teaching Timothy had received from Paul. How can

> I believe the single most significant decision I can make on a day-to-day basis is my choice of attitude. It is more important than my past, my education, my bankroll, my successes or failures, fame or pain, what other people think of me or say about me, my circumstances, or my position. Attitude keeps me going or cripples my progress. It alone fuels my fire or assaults my hope.
>
> —Charles R. Swindoll

doctrine stimulate us when we are discouraged? How does the Holy Spirit enable us to guard that good deposit? (Also see John 14:26 and John 16:13.)

Meditate on 2 Timothy 1:15–18

As Paul sits in prison how is he feeling? Can you relate a similar experience in your life? How did you overcome the despair of desertion?

In verses 16 to 18, Paul shares an example of true ministry. Why would Onesiphorus especially be appreciated by Paul? How can someone like Onesiphorus help us in times of discouragement?

Contemplation ✝ Reflect and Yield

How has discouragement paralyzed you in your spiritual walk? Do you want the Spirit of God to re-ignite you?

When have you been ashamed of sharing the gospel? Are you ready to allow the Lord to open opportunities for you to share your faith?

PRAYER ✝ RESPOND TO GOD

Read the sidebar quote from William Booth. Find a prayer partner, and share one thing that is discouraging you today. Pray that the fire on the altar of

> The tendency of fire is to go out; watch the fire on the altar of your heart.
>
> —General William Booth, founder of the Salvation Army

your hearts will not be extinguished and that you will find new confidence in Christ Jesus. Listen as God speaks words of encouragement to you.

INCARNATION ✝ LIVE THE WORD

What is one thing you can begin to do throughout this month to begin to rekindle your passion for living for Christ?

Pray that God will give you an opportunity to share the gospel message with someone this week. When the opportunity comes, seize it.

A WORKMAN APPROVED BY GOD

Listening for God through 2 Timothy 2:1–21

SUMMARY

In our everyday lives we look for products with the stamp of approval. We look for lights with a UL approval. We look for meat with a USDA approval. That stamp of approval guarantees us that the product is reliable.

We also seek approval for ourselves. We seek it from various sources and in various ways. We seek it from family and friends. We seek it in our professional lives. We seek it in our churches. As Christians we should be seeking God's approval above all others, but many times we aren't quite sure how to receive God's stamp of approval.

In this passage the Apostle Paul outlines some ways we might do this. As you study this passage, keep in mind that God wants to give His approval when you seek to please Him.

SILENCE ✝ LISTEN FOR GOD

One of God's titles in the Old Testament is *El Roi*, which means "the God who sees." Meditate on the truth that God sees all that you are and do.

PREPARATION ✝ FOCUS YOUR THOUGHTS

When you were young, whose approval did you most desire (for example, parent, coach, teacher, friend)? Why did you desire that person's approval?

READING ✝ HEAR THE WORD

This passage begins with an exhortation to Timothy to be strong in God's grace. This is a continuation of thought from chapter 1 in which Paul referred to his own suffering for the sake of the gospel. Watch for references to endurance, which is a central theme of this passage.

Especially note the three similes used to describe the ministry. This is one of many instances in his letters where Paul describes the Christian walk using military, athletic, and farming imagery.

Verses 11–13 are thought to be a hymn used in the early church. Especially note the "if" phrases, and whether each is negative or positive in content.

Examine this list of important terms:

Elect: This literally means *chosen*. It refers to all Christians who have faith in Christ.

Godless chatter: This phrase means *empty sounds,* probably referring to the doctrines of the false teachers.

Correctly handles: This term can also be translated *rightly dividing*. It means to cut straight.

Article: This refers to a container, vessel, or jar.

Read 2 Timothy 2:1–21.

MEDITATION ✝ ENGAGE THE WORD

Meditate on 2 Timothy 2:1–7

What is Paul's instruction to Timothy in verse 2? How did Timothy receive the gospel? (See 2 Tim. 1:5, 13.) How did you receive the gospel?

How would you define *endurance*?

Read the sidebar quote from Henry Ward Beecher. In what ways does enduring hardship develop Christian character and prepare us for better things?

> The little troubles and worries of life may be as stumbling blocks in our way, or we may make them stepping-stones to a nobler character and to Heaven. Troubles are often the tools by which God fashions us for better things.
> —Henry Ward Beecher

What are the three word pictures Paul uses to teach us about endurance?

In what ways is a Christian like a good soldier? How can you develop an attitude that sincerely wants to please the Lord above all other things?

Read the sidebar quote from Martha Graham. It also takes practice to become strong in God's grace. In what ways is the Christian life like running a race? What is the prize that is waiting for us at the end of the race?

> We learn by practice. Whether it means to learn to dance by practicing dancing or to learn to live by practicing living, the principles are the same. One becomes in some area an athlete of God.
> —Martha Graham, American dancer & choreographer

In what ways is a Christian like a farmer? How can we share in the crops of our spiritual harvest?

Meditate on 2 Timothy 2:8–13

Paul declares that the gospel is unchained even though he is chained in prison (v. 9). In what ways do you feel chained today? How can you unchain the gospel message in your life even though you might feel like you are in bondage?

Why does Paul willingly endure his sufferings? (See v. 10.) Why do you think he can say this with such confidence?

Read the sidebar quote from William Barclay. How is Paul turning his suffering into glory? What are you suffering today that you can allow God to turn into glory?

> Endurance is not just the ability to bear a hard thing, but to turn it into glory.
> —William Barclay

Review the "if" statements in verses 11–13. What do these phrases tell us about ourselves? About God? How does this hymn relate to the soldier, athlete, and farmer similes in verses

3–6? How does experiencing God's faithfulness encourage you to endure hardship?

Meditate on 2 Timothy 2:14–19

Who is the pronoun *them* referring to in verse 14? (See v. 2.) Why do Christians need to be reminded of certain truths to be effective teachers?

Why is quarreling about words of no value? In what ways does it ruin those who listen to the argument?

What is the model Paul sets forth in verse 15? How does being a workman approved by God keep you from being ashamed? How does this verse relate to 2 Timothy 1:7?

What is an approved workman able to do? What are some practical ways we can learn to correctly handle God's Word?

In what ways have you seen erroneous teaching spread like gangrene? What were the results of this? Scripture tells us that false teaching destroys faith. How does this encourage you to study God's truth for yourself?

Read the sidebar quote from Tim LaHaye. Why is studying God's Word such a chore for many Christians? Why are Christians afraid to study the Bible for themselves?

Meditate on 2 Timothy 2:20–21

What is the analogy we see in this section? The picture is that of articles in a home. What kinds of vessels are found there? What do they represent?

> A Greek mathematician once said, "There is no royal road to Geometry." This statement was made to a young student who wondered if there was an easier way of learning than study. As you know, there isn't, and the same is true for the Bible. In fact, it takes the hardest kind of work there is, thinking—but it is the only way it is ever learned.
>
> –Tim LaHaye

How does one become an instrument for noble purposes? (See verses 21–22.) Of what value is a vessel of honor? How can we determine whether we are being used for noble or ignoble purposes?

CONTEMPLATION ✟ REFLECT AND YIELD

What about your life would change if you would become a workman totally approved by God?

What are some things in your life you need to turn from in order to become a vessel of honor to God?

PRAYER ✟ RESPOND TO GOD

Which of the following do you most need to cultivate in your life: carrying out God's orders like a soldier; running by the Lord's rules rather than your own; or being diligent in God's work like a farmer?

Silently pray, confessing this need and listening for God's voice to encourage you.

INCARNATION ✟ LIVE THE WORD

God is calling you to become an athlete in your Christian walk. What will you begin to do today to train for this?

What steps will you take this week to further commit yourself to study God's Word? Who will you find to keep you accountable to this?

RECOGNIZING THE TRUTH

Listening for God through 2 Timothy 3:1–17

SUMMARY

Truth. It often seems like an elusive concept, constantly slipping through our grasp. Many believe truth is ever changing and that there is no such thing as absolute truth. Yet at the same time, we see people on a constant quest for absolute truth. Books, magazines, and TV introduce us to many who advertise their own brand of truth. We are being bombarded with conflicting ideologies all claiming to be truth. So how can we determine what is authentic?

As you consider this passage, remember that the discovery of truth was as elusive in the early church as it is today. As Paul presents a picture of what living in the last days entails, let it remind you of the world in which you live. Take comfort in the

fact that he offers concrete truths, genuine truths, to reward
our diligent search.

Silencia SILENCE ✝ LISTEN FOR GOD

God knows how confused we sometimes become. He sent His
Spirit to lead us into all truth (John 16:13). Listen to God's
voice assuring you that He will lead you into His truth.

Praeparatio PREPARATION ✝ FOCUS YOUR THOUGHTS

Relate a time when you have accepted erroneous teaching as
truth or were confused about the truth. How have you learned to
evaluate whether what you are hearing or reading is true or false?

Lectio READING ✝ HEAR THE WORD

As we read this passage, be especially aware of the contrasts
between evil men and godly men; false teaching and truth.
This passage also confronts readers with some important
teaching about the veracity of the Word of God.

Note the following terms:

Last days: In this context, this phrase refers to the days which began after Jesus' resurrection and continue until Christ's return to earth.

Jannes and Jambres: Jewish tradition identifies these as the magicians of Pharaoh's court who imitated Moses' miracles. (See Exodus 7:11.)

Antioch, Iconium and Lystra: These are cities in the Roman providence of Galatia where Paul encountered great persecution. He was stoned and left for dead in Lystra. Read Acts 13:13–14:21 for more details.

Training in righteousness: This kind of training helps people learn how to please God.

Read 2 Timothy 3:1–17.

MEDITATION ✦ ENGAGE THE WORD

Meditate on 2 Timothy 3:1–13

List the eighteen characteristics of living in the last days, as mentioned in verses 1–4. In what ways have you observed these characteristics in today's world?

What do you think Paul means when he describes people as "having a form of godliness but denying its power"? (See v. 5.) How can people appear to be of the truth yet never really experience truth?

Paul also mentions "weak-willed women" in this passage. What are three things that make them susceptible to erroneous teaching? What other factors make some people more gullible than others?

These women are described as loaded down with sins. How can guilt over our sins keep us from discovering truth? How can evil desires lead us to embrace error?

What does it mean to always learn but never come to the knowledge of the truth? (See v. 7.) In what ways do we see evidence of this in our world today?

Paul compares false teachers to Jannes and Jambres. What similarities do false teachers have to these men?

Read the sidebar quote from Matthew Henry. Do you believe seducers are more dangerous enemies to the church than persecutors? Why? How can a person know if he is being spiritually seduced or manipulated?

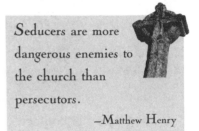

Seducers are more dangerous enemies to the church than persecutors.

—Matthew Henry

In verse 10 Paul states various facts about himself. What gives his message credibility?

The false teachers were seeking an easy life. What can a true believer expect in this life? How is Paul an example of this? Most of us will never be stoned because of our beliefs, yet how do we experience maltreatment because of our commitment to Christ? What can we do to prepare ourselves for the onslaught of this kind of treatment?

Meditate on 2 Timothy 3:14–17

What does Paul instruct Timothy to do in verse 14? What is the difference between learning truth and becoming convinced of truth? Why is having a conviction about our beliefs so important?

In verses 14–5, Paul gives us two ways to test what we are hearing. What are they?

How well do you know your teachers? Why is observing their lives imperative? Remembering that Scripture is the yardstick by which we can measure truth, how can we test the messages of visiting teachers and preachers or those with whom we have limited personal contact?

Read the sidebar quote from John R.W. Stott. Why is it important that we do not make relevance alone our standard of measure? Truth measured by relevance becomes subjective in nature. What is the problem with this?

> The modern world detests authority but worships relevance. Our Christian conviction is that the Bible has both authority and relevance, and that the secret of both is Jesus Christ.
>
> —John R.W. Stott

According to verse 15, what must accompany knowing God's Word? Why is faith in Christ needed to understand God's Word? How is Jesus Christ the secret to both relevance and authority?

What does it mean that Scripture is "God-breathed"? In Scripture, the breath of God often refers to the Holy Spirit. Read 1 Peter 1:21. What role did the Holy Spirit have in the inspiration of Scripture?

List and define the ways Scripture is useful. How have you found God's Word to be useful in your own life? In what ways does Scripture equip you for the work God has for you to do?

Contemplatio CONTEMPLATION ✝ REFLECT AND YIELD

Read the sidebar quote from Howard G. Hendricks. Is the Word conforming you into the image of Christ or are you being squeezed into the world's mold?

In what ways have you appeared godly, yet denied the power of God in your life?

> Dusty Bibles always lead to dirty lives. In fact, you are either in the Word and the Word is conforming you to the image of Jesus Christ, or you are in the world and the world is squeezing you into its mold.
>
> —Howard G. Hendricks

Oratio PRAYER ✝ RESPOND TO GOD

God desires that all people discover His truth. Gather in prayer clusters, and pray for one another that God would keep you from error and give you boldness to declare His truth. Listen for His voice promising to do this.

INCARNATION ✝ LIVE THE WORD

What one thing will you begin to do to guard yourself against spiritual manipulation?

Read the sidebar quote from Smith Wigglesworth. As you read God's Word this week, what will you do to ensure that you are becoming an "Epistle of God"? Keep a journal of your progress and praise God for your spiritual growth.

> God's Word is—Supernatural in origin; eternal in duration; inexpressible in valour; infinite in scope; regenerative in power; infallible in authority; universal in application; inspired in totality. Read it through, write it down; pray it in; work it out; pass it on. The Word of God changes a man until he becomes an Epistle of God.
>
> —Smith Wigglesworth

PASS IT ON

Listening for God through Titus 2:1–15

SUMMARY

As children we often had relay races. We would run our course and then pass the stick, ball, or other object to the next person until each one on the team had an opportunity to run. The Christian life is like a relay race. We have been entrusted with a faith that we must live out as well as pass on to others.

The Jews understood that we learn best from good examples. Jesus used this method to train His twelve disciples. They did not sit in a classroom and take notes from Jesus as He lectured. Rather they lived with and observed Jesus. The truths of the Kingdom were not only verbally taught by our Lord, but also demonstrated by Him in everyday life.

Each one of us has been called to pass on a living faith by word and example. As you meditate on this passage, consider how you can become a better model of your faith.

Silence ✝ Listen for God

Jesus came to earth to model how we should live. He calls us to follow His example. In silence, hear the voice of Jesus calling you to follow Him.

Preparation ✝ Focus Your Thoughts

List some of the people who made the greatest impact in your spiritual journey? In what ways were they an example to you? What lessons did you learn from them?

Reading ✝ Hear the Word

This letter was written to Titus, a Greek believer probably converted through the ministry of Paul. Titus appeared with Paul before the Jerusalem Council to testify of what God was doing among the Gentiles (Gal. 2:1–3). He was also a friend and a trusted colleague of Paul's (2 Cor. 7:5–16) who was given the task of delivering his second letter to the Corinthian church (2 Cor. 2:1–4).

At this point in church history, Titus had been sent to the island of Crete to finish Paul's work there (Titus 1:1). His job was to organize the church and develop a healthy congregation (1:5). The Cretans had earned a rather unflattering reputation (1:12), which presented additional challenges.

Paul begins the letter by outlining the qualifications for leadership and then instructs Titus how to relate to the various groups within the church. You will encounter the following terms in this passage:

Sound doctrine: This refers to healthy teaching. The theme of sound doctrine is consistent throughout the letters to Timothy and Titus. (See 1 Tim. 1:10, 6:3; 2 Tim. 1:13, 4:3; Titus 1:9, 13.)

Temperate: This calls believers to be balanced, moderate.

Self-controlled: This phrase calls believers to be sensible or clear-headed. (See Gal. 5:13–24.)

Be subject to: This does not mean to be forcibly submissive, but to yield voluntarily. Submission in Paul's letters never indicates inferiority. (See Eph. 5:24; 1 Peter 3:1, 5.)

Despise: This means to think beyond or depreciate.

Read Titus 2:1–15.

Meditation ✝ Engage the Word

Meditate on Titus 2:1–10

List the various groups Paul addresses in this section. How do we group believers in the church today? Many churches separate believers based on age, interest, or social situation. How can this be beneficial as well as detrimental to the church?

Read the sidebar quote from Ron Sider. Why is it important for believers of various ages and walks of life to share their lives with one another unconditionally?

> For the early Christians koinonia was not the frilly "fellowship" of church-sponsored bi-weekly outings. It was not tea, biscuits, and sophisticated small talk in the Fellowship Hall after the sermon. It was an unconditional sharing of their lives with the other members of Christ's body.
>
> –Ron Sider

What characteristics were the older men to pursue? The word *temperate* is often associated with drunkenness. However, the word means to be balanced in every area of life. How can older men become an example of balanced living to younger men today?

Read the sidebar quote from Paul Tournier. Older men were to be sound in faith, love, and endurance—qualities that reflect one's personal communion with God. How are these qualities contagious?

> Our task as laymen is to live our personal communion with Christ with such intensity as to make it contagious.
> —Paul Tournier

Cretans had to live down a stereotype of being liars, evil brutes, and lazy gluttons. What stereotypes do we have in the church today? How can they be overcome?

List the characteristics older women were to abandon. What were they to train the younger women to do? When you read the phrase "busy at home," what do you imagine? This term actually refers to managing the affairs of the home. Why would God desire women to be leaders in their homes?

In what ways are mothers the cog of the family wheel? How is being self-controlled, pure, and kind important in achieving this?

How can a modern woman be voluntarily submissive to her husband without becoming a doormat? How can women overcome feeling inferior when they are submissive?

How was Titus to teach the young men to be self-controlled? What characteristics was he to model? What else would be gained by being an example of godly living? How could Titus have been counter-productive if he had not been a man of integrity?

One group addressed is slaves. How is Paul speaking to this social system without condoning it? Why would he do this? List the ways slaves were to become examples to their masters. How can these principles be applied to workers and employers today?

Meditate on Titus 2:11–15

The first-century church lived with the expectation that Christ would return at any moment. Why have we lost much of this sense of anticipation in the church today? How can actively living with this hope become a motivation for us to be eager to do what is good?

What three things does Paul remind Titus to do in order to bring health to this local congregation? Knowing that this was a group of young believers, why would it be especially important for him to instill courage and correct them with authority?

Why was it important for Titus not to let anyone undermine his authority by trying to out think him or depreciate his position? Reflecting on this chapter, how could he to do this?

CONTEMPLATION ✝ REFLECT AND YIELD

Of which group listed are you a part? Of the qualities listed for your group, which do you need to develop?

Read the sidebar quote from Tim Elmore. How will you become more interdependent and less independent in relationship with others in your local fellowship?

> Americans cling to personal independence when they desperately need interdependence. God did not create people to be self-sufficient and move through life alone. To return to healthy relational living will require recognition of this need and courage to change.
>
> –Tim Elmore

PRAYER ✝ RESPOND TO GOD

Pray for one another so that you might become better examples of Christ to each other. Also pray that God would instill a sense of urgency in you for becoming a living example of His love.

INCARNATION ✝ LIVE THE WORD

Identify one person from whom you can learn more about the Christian life and one person whom you can mentor about living for Christ. This week develop a plan to build ongoing relationships with these people.

DEVOTED TO DOING GOOD

Listening for God through Titus 3:1–15

SUMMARY

It is easy for us, as Christians, to build a shell around ourselves to protect us from the world and its evil ways. Instead of hiding from the world, we have a duty to model the Christian faith openly and in practical ways.

Christians have been accused of being so heavenly minded that they are no earthly good. That is, at times we focus too much on doctrine and theology and neglect to flesh out our faith. The Lord chastised the Jews because they strictly adhered to the law but neglected justice and mercy (Matt. 23:23). Are we any different?

As Paul closed this short letter to Titus, he admonished Christians to live in the world peaceably and with humility. The assurance of our eternal destiny frees us to add to and not subtract from the world. It liberates us to live each day devoted to doing great things in the name of Christ.

As you study, allow the Lord to challenge you to live a more productive life for His Kingdom in the world in which you live.

SILENCE ✝ LISTEN FOR GOD

Jesus completely devoted himself to do the Father's will. You are called to do the same. Listen to the Lord calling you to yield yourself completely to Him.

PREPARATION ✝ FOCUS YOUR THOUGHTS

How would you define the word *devotion?* How can you tell if a person is devoted to something? What things are you devoted to? Why?

Lectio READING ✝ HEAR THE WORD

In chapter 2 Paul addressed how believers are to interact with the household of faith. In this passage he addresses our witness to an unbelieving world.

Watch for the phrase, *devoted to doing good.* Note the various contexts in which this phrase occurs.

Paul balances his exhortation to do whatever is good by highlighting God's kindness, love, and mercy as the means for our salvation. Salvation is not earned but is a free gift. (See Eph. 2:1–10.) Note how God has saved you as you read this passage.

Also note the names of church leaders in this passage. Either Artemas or Tychicus will be sent to Crete to replace Titus. According to 2 Timothy 4:12, we know Tychicus will later be sent by Paul to replace Timothy in Ephesus. Apollos is a well-known figure in the church. See Acts 18:23–28; 1 Corinthians 3:1–7 and 16:12 for more background on these individuals.

Review these important terms:

Foolish: This refers to a spiritual foolishness, rather than a worldly one.

Washing of rebirth: This refers to how the Old Testament priests washed in the laver in the Temple to cleanse themselves. When we are born-again, our sins are washed away (John 3:5–8; Heb. 10:22).

Renewal by the Holy Spirit: This phrase refers to the ongoing work of the Holy Spirit of making the believer new. (Rom. 12:2; 1 Cor. 4:16–18).

Justified by grace: This speaks of being declared righteous before God and accepted by Him based on Christ's completed work on the cross not our works.

Read Titus 3:1–15.

MEDITATION ♱ ENGAGE THE WORD

Meditate on Titus 3:1–2

List the things Titus was to remind the people to do in verse 1.

In what ways were the Cretans to submit themselves to authorities? In what practical ways can we be good citizens today?

Verse 2 talks about godly actions in our relationships. List some of the characteristics of a godly relationship.

To be peaceable means to avoid quarreling. What is a better way of handling disagreements? Christ calls us to be peacemakers

(Matt. 5:9). What is the difference between peacemaking and peacekeeping?

How would you define "true humility toward all men"?

Read the sidebar quote from Phillips Brooks. How does humility enable the power of God to be revealed in your life? True humility begins with taking an honest evaluation of yourself. Why is it so hard for us to be honest with ourselves?

> No man or woman of the humblest sort can really be strong, gentle, pure, and good without the world being better for it, without somebody being helped and comforted by the very existence of that goodness.
>
> —Phillips Brooks

Meditate on Titus 3:3–8

List the character traits we all had before we came to Christ, as outlined by Paul in verse 3. Why is Paul reminding us that everyone has vices?

In contrast, list the characteristics of God in the work of salvation. According to this passage, what has God done for us?

How would you define the phrases *washing of rebirth, renewal by the Holy Spirit,* and *justified by grace?* Why would Titus need to stress these things?

Read the sidebar quote from Wesley Duewel. To devote ourselves to doing good, what might it cost us? Although doing good has its cost, it also brings rewards. What are they? What other incentives do people have for doing good works?

> Today most Christians have a very cheap understanding of what it means to be a disciple. Today the average Christian lifestyle costs almost nothing. Jesus wants followers who are willing to volunteer to pay a price, to be willing to suffer, if need be, for Him. This is the holy commitment that He wants to characterize your spiritual lifestyle.
>
> —Wesley Duewel

Meditate on Titus 3:9–15

What is Paul's instruction to Titus in verse 9? Note that this is the same instruction Paul gave to Timothy. (See 1 Tim. 1:3–5.)

Devotion to doing good also includes striving for unity within the body of Christ. This unity was the subject of Jesus' prayer in John 17, so clearly it was a pivotal issue. Why is unity within the church important as we relate to the world? What unprofitable issues divide the church today?

Read the sidebar quote from Dick Mills. Why is it important for Christians to work together as a team? How does a *prima donna*, Lone Ranger, or superstar attitude contribute to divisions within the church?

> Christianity is not for soloists, prima donnas, lone rangers, heavyweights, or superstars. None of us is a law unto himself or herself. We must work together as a team to represent Christ to the uncommitted.
>
> —Dick Mills

How was Titus instructed to handle a divisive person? Why was he instructed to do this? In what ways is a divisive person self-condemned? What are some practical ways the church can handle those who cause strife and divisions?

What is Paul asking Titus to do in verse 13? What are some practical ways we can help Christian servants such as missionaries and traveling speakers?

Paul begins verse 14 with the phrase "our people." This indicates that devotion to doing good is the responsibility of the entire church. What are the two benefits he mentions of being devoted to doing what is good? Paul ends his letter by praying God's grace be with them. How does the grace of God help us remain devoted to doing good?

CONTEMPLATION ✝ REFLECT AND YIELD

Look at your life before Christ and what God has done since your conversion. How can the change you've experienced become an incentive to devote yourself to doing good?

Are you ready to make a new commitment or renew your devotion to fulfilling God's command to live out your faith in practical ways?

PRAYER ✝ RESPOND TO GOD

Read the sidebar quote from Francis Schaeffer. In silent prayer, ask God to show you how you can be more devoted to living under His Lordship. Listen to His voice telling you that there are no little people in His Kingdom.

> Those who think of themselves as little people in little places, if committed to Christ and living under His Lordship in the whole of life, may, by God's grace, change the flow of our generation.
>
> —Francis Schaeffer

Incarnation ✝ Live the Word

Meditate on your past life and what God has done for you since your salvation. Then write a letter of thanksgiving to God, telling Him of your new resolve to live a productive life for His Kingdom.

Ask God to show you someone you can help this week in a practical way.

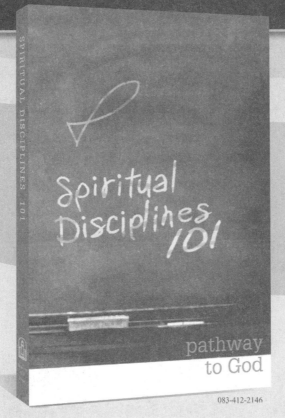

Experience Greater Intimacy With God!

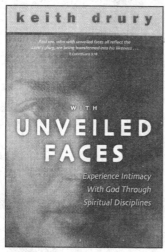

With Unveiled Faces

Experience Intimacy With God Through Spiritual Disciplines

By Keith Drury

0-89827-298-X
Paperback

$12.99
160 pages

Nurture your relationship with God as you experience each of these personal spiritual disciplines:

- Prayer
- Silence
- Study
- Fasting
- Obedience
- Simplicity
- Giving
- Sacrifice
- Serving
- Meditation
- Journaling
- Self-denial
- Solitude

Each chapter of the book introduces the discipline, explains the biblical background, gives practical tips for practicing the discipline, and ends with questions for discussion and follow up.

Order today from your local Christian bookstore!

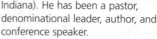

KEITH DRURY teaches practical ministry at Indiana Wesleyan University (Marion, Indiana). He has been a pastor, denominational leader, author, and conference speaker.